The Lucky Rescue Mom and Her Forgotten Five

Susan Kraus

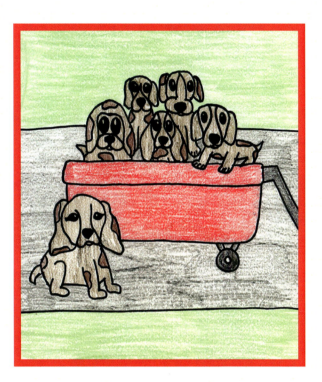

Second in the series,
"Because That's What Susie Does"
This series of books features stories which teach your child compassion for all living things. They are able to receive the intended message while participating in the rescues and becoming part of the story.

**Illustrations by
Karli and Kaitlyn Mullins, Animal-Loving Kids**

A portion of the proceeds will benefit
animal shelters and rescue groups.

The Lucky Rescue of Mom and Her Forgotten Five

©Susan Kraus 2014

Illustrated by Animal Loving Kids,
Karli and Kaitlyn Mullins

ISBN: 978-1-63110-00000

All Rights Reserved Under
International and Pan-American Copyright Conventions.
No part of this book may be used or reproduced in any manner
whatsoever without written permission except in the case of brief
quotations embodied in critical articles or reviews.

Mira Digital Publishing
Chesterfield, Missouri 63005

Thanks to all the **special people** who have supported me, had confidence in me and allowed me to publish this second book. Your skills, wisdom and kindness do not go unnoticed.

I dedicate my second book to the many **animals** that have experienced abuse at the hands of humans. May the victims find peace and the abuser find compassion.

Susie and some of her animals.
(Not everyone would participate!)

Hi Kids,

It's Susie again. First, let me say "thank you" for liking my first book. Because of you, I was allowed to write book two. That's pretty cool.

Secondly, I would like to think you know now how much I love animals. I know you must love them too.

Have fun reading and learning about a man who had to learn a lesson about his dog. Maybe after you read this book, you too could start helping people understand how important it is to be kind to animals.

Susie

This is a true story.

I hope you enjoy it.

Mommy and
her forgotten five
were lucky dogs,

but they didn't know it yet.

"Mommy, I'm so hot!
My tummy hurts!
Mommy, I'm thirsty!"

It was a very hot summer day.
Susie was working out in the yard.
As she came around the front
to water her plants,
she suddenly stopped...

"What is that sound?"
Susie whispered to herself.
She listen more closely.

"YIPE, YIPE, YIPE,"
was all she heard.

YIPE!! YIPE!!! YIPE! YIPE!!

Susie knew that sound was coming from dogs that were in trouble.

"Where are you little ones?"

She called out. "Help me find you!"

YIPE! YIPE!!! YIPE! YIPE!! YIPE!!

...Because, That's What Susie Does!

"YIPE, YIPE, YIPE."

The sound kept getting louder
and louder. Susie followed it
to the backyard of the
house across the road.

"OH MY GOODNESS!"
She shouted when she saw
what was causing the sound.

There, huddled in a very small cage
barely big enough to move,
was a mommy beagle dog
and five very young puppies.

The sun was very hot
and beating down on them.
The cage had little shelter
from the sun,
no food and no water.

"How could anyone do this to you?"

Susie was crying now.

"I don't know what to do first," she mumbled, but she quickly figured it out.

...Because, That's What Susie Does!

Question Time...

Should Susie just sit and pet the dogs?

OR

Should she get them to a cool spot until she could figure out the best thing to do?

If you said "get them to a cool place until she could figure out the best thing to do," good for you!

Give yourself a pat on the head.

Susie immediately went to work.

She noticed that one
of the puppies was barely moving,
so Susie had to move fast.

She ran as quickly as
her legs would carry her,
back to her house.

She got her red wagon
and went zooming
back to the dogs.

She was running so fast,
her red wagon looked like
it was flying behind her.

"I'm coming guys, hang on!"
Susie yelled.

Her legs hurt from running so fast.
When she got there,
Susie quickly lifted
the five puppies out
of the cage and gently laid
each one in her little red wagon.

Then Susie gently lifted
Mom out of the cage,
kissed her head and
whispered in her ear,
"You are safe now Mommy.
I'll take care of you and your babies."

...Because, That's What Susie Does!

Susie, the five puppies and their mommy headed back to Susie's house. When she got them in her backyard, Susie looked at the sick puppy and knew what to do.

She sat on the step of her swimming pool with the puppy on her lap.

Question Time...

Should Susie dunk
the puppy into the water?

or
Should she keep him on
her lap and slowly dribble cool
water on the puppy's body?

Hopefully you said
keep the puppy on her lap
and **<u>dribble</u>** cool water on his body.
We never want to put
a puppy into water
without an adult present, right?

Susie loves that you
are so smart about animals.
Give yourself a life preserver
for saving this puppy.

So Susie did just that and
slowly began dripping water
onto his body. Susie just knew the
puppy had gotten way too hot.

When the puppy started feeling
better, Susie started cheering.
The other puppies began jumping
around and barking.
Susie laughed with delight.

After all the excitement was over,
Susie realized what she
had done while saving the lives of
mommy and her puppies.

She had taken someone else's dogs!
Susie frowned.
"Now what?" she moaned.

A few days later, the owner came home and Susie immediately walked over, introduced herself and explained what had happened.

Susie was shocked when the man said, "I really don't care."

The man whose name was Jake, explained his dogs were like his tools and he only used them for jobs. He wanted the mom for hunting but said, "I definitely don't want those pups."

Susie knew it was time to help this man understand that animals do have feelings and are nothing like tools.

…Because, That's What Susie Does!

Question Time...

Do you agree with Susie that animals have feelings?

or

Do you agree with Jake that they are only good when work needs to be done?

Let's hope you said you agree with Susie. If you did, then you are a compassionate person. That means you care.

Give yourself a high paw!

Susie very politely suggested
the two of them talk more about
animals. She then offered
to take care of mommy and the puppies
until they were ready for homes.
Jake loved that idea!

Susie started for home scratching
her head. "They are like your tools?"
She kept repeating to herself,
not believing he could really think that!

Susie kept her promise and
visited Jake as much as she could.
They talked about lots of things,
but mostly she explained
how animals have feelings.

"They feel things like hunger
and thirst, heat and cold, happiness,
pain and loneliness, just like we do."

Susie explained to Jake
all the ways animals help us.

Question Time...

Can you name one way animals help us?

I bet you thought of a lot of kind ways animals help us. There are so many.

Give yourself a wag of the tail!

Susie told Jake stories about hero dogs that saved their owners from fires and drowning.

She told him about the dogs that helped find loved ones after a disaster, like 911, tornadoes and hurricanes.

Susie told the story of how a cat went into a burning fire to rescue all seven of her kittens, one by one.

Susie even took Jake to a training place for dogs that help adults and children who aren't able to do certain things for themselves. They are children who can't walk or can't see or even can't talk.

"These dogs are so smart, Jake!" Susie said.
"These are called Therapy Dogs."

"The stories go on and on." Susie explained.

Jake began to understand a little and he actually asked how his mom dog was doing. Susie smiled to herself and thought, "it's working!"

Soon the puppies were 8 weeks of age and old enough to go to their new homes.

Question Time...

Should Susie take them to a shopping center parking lot and just give them away as people come out of the store?

or

Should Susie contact all her animal-loving friends and have them help her find good, responsible homes?

If you said have her friends help, you are correct and caring.

Give yourself a "Yippie!"

Susie knew she had to be sure the puppies went to responsible pet owners. She knew she would carefully check out each home.

...Because,
That's What Susie Does!

This also meant it was time to
let their mommy go back to Jake.

Susie felt Jake would
be better to her now.
Jake said he understood now and
would take better care of her.

He also promised to make sure
she didn't have any more puppies!
Susie felt good and thought their
talks worked.

Jake had one more thing
to ask his new friend, Susie.
"I want to rename my dog after you.
Would that be okay?"

Susie smiled really big.
"I guess that would be okay."

They both laughed.

"Everybody's lucky now!" Susie said.

Meet the Real Mom dog and her five puppies.

Also, thanks to the new owners, here they are grown up!
(no picture of #5)

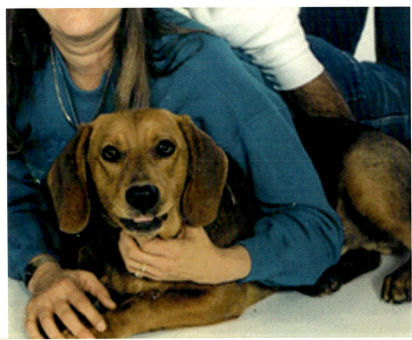

Parents,

Let me first thank you for giving your child this gift of learning.

Second and beyond, please be aware of any opportunity to help any animal in need. It's a great lesson of compassion for your child as well as yourself. Whenever the opportunity presents itself, educate those who do not understand responsible pet ownership. Be kind but persistent.

I would like to think your pet, if you have one, is spayed or neutered. Some people think it's un-natural, not manly or not fair to fix them. Please realize, what is not fair is heightening the females risk of breast and ovarian cancer and in males, prostate cancer. Hormones in both sexes will accelerate about the age of two and some dogs may become more assertive at that time.

Remember, we domesticated these animals 1000s of years ago and took away the natural balance of nature. We have created, therefore, a tremendous pet over-population of unwanted and homeless dogs and cats. Shelters and rescue groups are bursting at the seams with more and more relinquished pets and fewer and fewer adoptions.

Cats and kittens are brought into shelters (those that will accept them) by the truck loads with no home to adopt them. Diseased and emaciated dogs and cats are walking our streets looking for just a morsel of food or a drink of water. This is the human's fault. Please do not continue to add to the heart wrenching and uncontrolled problem.

Many shelters today offer payment plans and low cost spay and neuter. (One low rate comes from St. Louis' Carol House Quick Fix clinic, 314-771-7387 [PETS] or visit their website at www.CarolHousePetClinic.org.) There is no longer any excuse to not help stop the tremendous pet over-population and neglect of the victims.

Thank you for sharing this story with your young ones and for teaching them compassion towards all two and four-legged friends.

Susie